FROM MY
MOUTH
TO YOUR
EAR

FROM MY MOUTH TO YOUR EAR

ORIGINAL WORKS OF POETRY

CHOCOLATE SISTAH

PRIMIX
PUBLISHING
THE WRITE CHOICE

Primix Publishing
11620 Wilshire Blvd
Suite 900, West Wilshire Center, Los Angeles, CA, 90025
www.primixpublishing.com
Phone: 1-800-538-5788

Published by Primix Publishing: 07/13/2023

ISBN: 978-1-957676-73-9(sc)
ISBN: 978-1-957676-74-6(e)

Library of Congress Control Number: 2023912083

CONTENTS

Dedication ix

1 LOVE 1
Achieve 2
Advantage 3
Allow 4
Alone. 6
And I Call You FRIEND 8
As Many... 9
Balancing Act 10
Barren. 11
Beacon 12
Big City, Bright Lights. 13
Bow and Arrow 14
Breathless 15
Change 16
Choices 17
Contradictions. 18
Courage 19
Cravin' 20
Cry 21
Cut to the Quick. 22
Daddy's Little Girl. 23
Determined. 24
Don't Steal My Joy 25
Don't Sweat the Small Stuff. 26
DREAM 27
Drownin'. 28
Emotional 29
FASHIONISTA 30

Feel Good 31

Female. 32

Friendship 33

From My Mouth to Your Ear. 34

Hate 35

Heart. 36

Heavy on My Mind. 37

Hopeful. 38

How Does It Feel 39

Hypocrite 40

I Love Me Some You 41

If. 42

Innocence Lost 43

Innuendo. 45

Instigate 46

Life Change. 47

Little Pond 48

Livin' Large 49

Love is. 50

Love Ya Like a Play Cousin 51

LURE. 52

Male 53

Me 54

Murphy's Law 55

My Hero 56

Naked 57

Nothing Else Said 58

On Angels' Wings. 59

Power 61

Ray of Light 62

Reflection 63

Sacrifice. 64

Same Like Me 65

Save the World 67

Shades. 68

She is..69

Shine...70

Sing My Soul......................................71

Sistah Girl, Sistah Friend 72

Skin Deep...73

Smile...74

SOLITUDE 75

Sorry for What 76

Soul Food 78

Speak!..79

Still...80

Suddenly..81

Sunshine..82

Teach 83

Tears 84

THE "DO"..85

The Verdict.......................................86

The Vow of Marriage 87

They Turn into Angels 88

Those Who...89

Thumbs Up! 90

Touch 91

TRIUMPH...92

Trust.... Yourself................................93

Ultimate 94

Unbelievable 95

Why Me?...96

You Grandmother 97

You 99

About the Author 101

DEDICATION

I want to dedicate this book, this piece of my heart and soul to my late father, Wilbur L. Fleming, and grandmother Evelyn C. Phillips to show them I did follow my dream and didn't give up. I know they are both proud of me and are looking down from their watch tower with a smile on their face. I also want to give a special thanks to my husband Anthony who proofread my poetry and gave me the moral support I needed to go forward. Last, but certainly not least, is to my mother, Laura B. Fleming, my biggest cheerleader who inspired me to reach my fullest potential. Much love to all of those who always believed in me.

I know I want to go places and hope you are there to enjoy the ride of a lifetime.

1 LOVE

You are my main squeeze –
    You are the yin to my yang
        The up to my down
            The wind to my sail
                The end to my beginning
                    The start to my finish

You are the sun to my sky
    The roses to my bouquet
        The flowers to my garden
            The bubbles to my bubble bath

You are the pot of gold to my rainbow
    The ray of sun after my rain shower
        The dandelions to my open fields

You are the butter to my toast
    The skillet to my grilled cheese sandwich
        The preserves to my mason jar

You are not only the hot fudge, you are the
            whole sundae
You are my one and only – my 1 love!

ACHIEVE

You are what I aspire to be
If I set the bar any higher,
God herself wouldn't be able to
Reach where I have placed it
Even now, the standard may
Still be too high
But that's okay
Because I tell myself I am
Worth every sleepless night
And
Every needless worry
I do admit I over compensate
At times, become over anxious,
Even down right greedy
I want everything
NOW
My inspiration is YOU
And
YOU change every day
It ALL seems possible
Do able!

ADVANTAGE

Third time is a charm
Behind every dark cloud, there's a silver lining
When one door closes, another one opens
The grass is greener…
You must kiss a lot of frogs…

When life hands you lemons, make lemonade
He's a diamond in the rough
Don't make a mountain out of a molehill
Don't cut off your nose to spite your face

Life can have many twists and turns, many uncertainties
You can play your hand ever so carefully, by dotting every "i" and
Crossing every "t", yet you are still bound to miss something, to
Overlook even the tiniest of details

By taking advantage of the present moment, the here and now, there are
No missed opportunities, no room for error
The grass stays greener; the lemonade is always flowing
There are no frogs to kiss and the roads are always straight without any
unnecessary roadblocks

The advantage to living life conquers any ill will of destroying it!

ALLOW

I won't allow our children
To see you through a plexi-glass window
Or
Say hello to you
Through a telephone
On the prison wall

I won't allow myself
To say hello to you
Or
Feel your touch through
Prison bars

I won't allow you
To be seen as less of
A king
Than you are
By
Being dragged off to
A holding cell
And treated like you
Are non-human

I won't allow it

I have choices and
I choose not to be a
Victim
Victim of change or
Circumstance

I choose to be a
Strong woman

I will choose a man
Who loves me unconditionally
By making correct decisions
For himself
As well as for us

I choose to live life
By living right
And leave toxic people
Where I found them

What I want is what
I allow
And I allow myself
To be happy
With or without
You

I allow myself
To be happy
With myself
With help from
My self

ALONE

Cryin' into the covers to muffle the sound
Not wanting to speak to anyone, but knowing you should
talk to someone – someone who has your best interest
at heart; someone who won't judge
You know you should 'spill the beans' on yourself, but
you haven't found the courage to break the silence –
to ask for help
Tryin' to push to the back of your mind what people
will think of you – how harshly they will judge you,
thinkin' that you can't hold it together; thinkin' you
are weak; could they be right?
Pushin' to the back of your mind the guilty pleasure
you feel when you do feel sorry for yourself
Givin' yourself permission to comfort yourself; taking
that extra attention you feel no one else is giving you
Then reality sinks in
Again
The tears start to flow
Again
Your eyes turn that bright red after a good and hard cry
Your lids so heavy, they feel and look more like mini
pillows than a fixture on your face
Whatever is going on, it is difficult to think anyone
will understand what you are going through
How can they? Don't they understand this is the worst
you've felt, the most pain you've been in?
Don't they know it is your RIGHT to cry, to feel down,
to feel sorry for yourself?
So you cry into the covers to muffle the sound
wanting so badly for someone to walk in and
comfort you – but they don't
You cry until you have no more tears to cry; you

drift off to sleep
You get over it
Until
The next time
The next situation

AND I CALL YOU FRIEND

I consider you my true friend
Confidante
At times you appear at the BEST possible moment
or call me so I can hear your voice to let me know you were thinking of me
The little things you do mean so much and how you view me as someone
you care about touches me in such a way it is difficult for me to describe
Being crazy and finishing each other's sentences are some of the few things
I LOVE about you FRIEND; those silly events are more than just fringe
benefits, they're part of the WHOLE package when it comes to you
Kind-hearted
Sincere
Stern (when need be)
Gentle
Funny
Smart
I have learned so much from you and I consider it a privilege to have you be a
part of my life
You keep me levelheaded but give me enough rope so I won't be able to hurt
myself too badly
We have a SOLID foundation, which has stood the test of time; phone calls,
which
have been few and far between, but NEVER lose the excitement when we DO
connect, we don't skip a beat! Always there for one another to share important
milestones in our lives or small ones including being each other's moral support
I consider you my true friend in every sense of the word
And I call you friend NOW and FOREVER!

AS MANY...

As many stars there are in the sky
As many blades of grass are in the meadows
As many grains of sand on all the shores
As many fish there are in the oceans
Pales in comparison to your glowing smile

As many secret languages being spoken
As many shades of skin populating the earth
As many paths leading to the Holy Land
As many prayers being answered by the Almighty every day
As many angels who are looking down on their loved ones, protecting them
Doesn't come close to the way I feel about you
My love which I give freely because you love wholly

BALANCING ACT

There can't be night without day
Rain without sunshine
Good without bad
Positive without negative
Big without small
Tall without short
Rich without poor

Is it possible for the unliked to be liked
The sad to be happy
The unlucky in love to find that special someone
The depressed to be content
The hated to be forgiven
The naïve to con

In life there is a cycle,
  A beginning and an end A balancing act to keep
Everything in its place; to keep things running smoothly

In life there are pros and cons,
                    Which side are you on?

BARREN

Barren
Bare, non-producing
Nothing "Ripe" at time of harvest
Thought things would go better, turn out differently
Barren
Baring NOTHING
NO
MORALITY
COMMON SENSE
SENSIBILITY
LOVE
Do not only think of someone NOT being able to
"conceive" when you think of "barren"
Think of your own land
You can actually be "barren" without even knowin'
it
Walkin' down the street feelin' fine
but
Empty INSIDE
Missing something, not complete
Think of the fertility you have
and
How actually fertile you REALLY are
Make sure the two MATCH
by
Measuring the same components
Be full of something
Hopefully –
LIFE!

Beacon

You always have the light on to show me the way
You know how to right my wrongs and turn my frowns into smiles
You allow me to be my own person
But
At the same time, work at removing stubborn obstacles directly blocking my path, my growth
Your light shines brightly like a beacon
Your spirit transformed into a star guiding me in the right direction high from the night's sky
Disguising yourself to ensure my protection
My faith keeps you close at hand
My genuine prayers make it easier for you to grant my requests
My beacon of light, my lifesaver
The One I can count on the most, without any hesitation
The light of my life
The one I can't live without because without you my life would be empty and meaningless
Believing in you wholeheartedly is a worthwhile investment
The end result being eternal life with Him and his angels

BIG CITY, BRIGHT LIGHTS

As I look into the night's sky
The skyline bright with wonder, with mystery – what secrets lie here?
Who did what to whom to get where they are today?
How many hearts have been broken, how many pipe dreams went up in
smoke to build these skyscrapers, these buildings that reach the heavens?
What lies between these bricks and mortar?
Blood, sweat, and tears were the least of the things given up for the growth
of this city
Trailblazers cut out a piece of history and made it their own
Today, it is the turn of the youth to blaze our future
The skyline bright with wonder, with a destination in mind, in sight
The path we take, the path we build is not only up to us, it is left to us
Without carefully choosing a path
Without building upon what is already in existence, we are in grave danger
of losing a generation and eventually losing ourselves forever
Big city, brighter future
We have the world on a string!

BOW AND ARROW

The love bandit has hit me
Shot by cupid's arrow
Not right between the eyes
but
Straight in the heart
On the first try
Bull's eye!

I've been changed by the bow and arrow
Cupid decided my life needed rearranging and
Took the proper measures to do so
Something for the better
Changed by the direction of the bow

I was an unsuspecting target
A guaranteed hit
Cupid took aim, pointed and fired
There hasn't been one yet that he has let get
away
Once you're in his sight, it's over
He never misses

BREATHLESS

You take my breath away
Every time I look at you
Your eyes, your smile, the way you gently touch my hand
Sends shivers up and down my spine
You have a hold on me without doing a thing
To think I thought I'd be alone forever, with no one to love me
Then you came along
Sweet, sincere and wise beyond your years
When it comes to matters of the heart
You take my breath away
But what you don't know is I would have gladly given it to you, freely
I don't know what I did to deserve you, so I won't second-guess the outcome
I will be overjoyed with my good fortune for the rest of my life
My life with you!

CHANGE

Change is necessary
When things aren't going in a direction you wish
Change is beneficial
For you to move forward
Change is good
To cleanse the soul
Change is bad
If you have to compromise your principles
Change is damaging
If you are asked to hurt yourself in the process
Change is healthy
When it is done to better the individual
Change is positive
When it is recognized to be helpful
The world changes on a moment to moment basis and we
Change with it, whether we want to or not
Change is consistent and being stagnant
Doesn't negate the fact that
Change is happening
It's happening all around you
Without any warning
Without any apologies

CHOICES

A lifetime of experiences played out by a lifetime of learning to trust your own
Decisions

NEVER neglected by those who mean something to you, but being guilty of
Neglecting your own needs by making rash impulsive mistakes

Yes, there are many things, which could influence and even interfere with
the path

In which the journey begins and without even knowing it, the course takes an
Unexpected turn with you falling victim to being content

By actually regaining the reins and believing in yourself again, you knew
which was

Clearly the correct path for you to take

You became focused and more determined than you ever thought possible

When you come to an impasse, the proverbial fork in the road

You first must choose the course, believe in it, NOT haphazardly, but
wholeheartedly

Equating the ACTION with that of blind faith

Shining the light on what is actually taking place NOT on egos trying to
take credit

The age-old debate raging back and forth in your mind is whether the choice
you've

Made is worth the price it takes to change it

CONTRADICTIONS

Raining when the sun is shining
Smiling when you feel like crying
Embracing your enemy after they have wronged you
Blowing off responsibilities instead of going to work
Doing something for someone when it's least expected
Being middle aged and not looking a day over 21

The world is full of contradictions seen and unseen
Understandable and mind boggling
Life moves forward with or without you, it is never stagnant,
Constantly in motion
Contradictions, you make the decision whether they become positive
Contradictions, the driving force behind the actions we take regardless of
the degree of involvement

COURAGE

What does it mean to be courageous?
To fight off those trying to harm you, your family?
To speak out when it is not in vogue to go against
the status quo?
To stand up and veer to the left when everyone
is comfortable staying right?

Being courageous is not just showing your
muscle but also showing your demeanor

Carrying a big stick without a precedence
for violence
Having a commanding voice without shouting
Showing leadership ability without being
forceful
Creating a following without demanding a
crowd

What does it mean to have courage?

Being the best person you can be without
selling yourself to conformity

CRAVIN'

You are my morning fix
The way you wake me with a kiss

You are my afternoon craving
Hearing your voice in the middle of the day
Makes me want you here and now

In the evening, I can't wait to see you; I've been
Without you ALL day and I need you bad, really
I do!
You got me fiendin' and there's no cure for it and I'm glad!

You got me so wound up I can't see straight; your lovin' is
Like a drug and I can never get too much of you; when you touch
Me, you give me my dose but it leaves me wanting more

It's hard to describe what you do to me, BUT don't stop; I'm fixed
On you for life – I will CRAVE you for the rest of my life!

CRY

Cry
to cleanse your mind
Whimper
to disguise what is happening at the moment
Cry
hard so you don't have to feel
Cry
at sentimental things
Cry
to show your sensitive side
Cry
whether you are male or female
Cry
to show you are human
Cry
just for the sake of crying
Cry
so you know you can get in touch with what is deep inside of you
Crying
doesn't make you weak; in fact, crying gives you a sense of strength
Don't
be afraid to show you are moved in a way that doesn't fit the norm
Cry
to show you beat to your own drum
Be
yourself
Cry

CUT TO THE QUICK

One sharp slip of the tongue
One sweet word spoken in a tone that can bring a tear to your eye
The lesser of two evils
Or
The curse of the moment at hand

"I love you" followed by an
"I hate you"
Both legitimate feelings
Both having merit
Both cutting like a knife
Both can be taken at face value

The tongue can speak so eloquently
Yet
Tear a person down to nothing
In a split second
The cut of the tongue
You can decide which way
To use it to your
Advantage

DADDY'S LITTLE GIRL

Always wanting to please you, never wanting to disappoint you
Wanting to follow in your footsteps, the youngest but striving to be the strongest
Wanting in every way to be like you, a gentle giant
Love unconditionally
Delegate with ease
Give orders firmly
Live life to the fullest
Treating each day as if you were a sponge, soaking up whatever is around you
Not giving much thought to the fact I was the female filling the shoes of a
Great male as I stare at myself through your reflection
I never thought anything was out of my grasp because you taught me to aim high
I always knew I would amount to something because you taught me never to give
Up on myself and pushed me to be my best
I never felt inferior because you taught me that I am a superior person
Daddy, when I look at you I see me
Daddy, when I talk you speak
Daddy, whenever I need consoling you are always there
Even when you showed your temper, Daddy, I knew I was loved
As I stand before you as a woman today
Daddy,
I will always and forever be your little girl

DETERMINED

What determines a state of mind?
Who, among the masses,
is qualified
to make that judgement
call

Taking a stand
making a decision
Determining that your opinion
is worth weighing
in
Determining that your worth
is worth
while

Searching for worthy causes
something to lend your name
to
which will raise more
than just
eyebrows
Making sure that by deeming something
"good"
it is determined to be
as such

Don't Steal My Joy

Don't steal my joy
The joy that I set aside for my pure pleasure
The joy that I need when I am not feeling myself
The joy that I have placed on reserve, the joy I use when I am at my lowest
Yes, that joy
It might seem petty to you, but I rely on this
particular joy to get me out of some
Sticky situations
Joy to keep me normal
Joy to keep me sane
Please, if you have stolen any part of my joy
I beg you to return it to me as soon as possible
Since I rely so heavily on my joy, maybe to the point of obsession
It would be a good idea to replace what was taken with no questions asked
Because I would be a better person with it
It, meaning JOY!

DON'T SWEAT THE SMALL STUFF

Do you ever think anything is "small stuff"?
Someone cutting in front of you after waiting over an hour
in line
Someone not holding the door for you when they know you
were directly in back of them
Someone not saying "thank you" when they know you have
done something to benefit them?
When do you become the "bigger person" and not let the
"small stuff" get out of hand?
When does taking the higher road benefit the road seeker?
When does turning the other cheek not sting when it is slapped?
The answer to these burning questions might be hidden in the
stars, but I do believe that by not sweating the things that can
spin out of control, we can concentrate on keeping what we do
have control over on its axis

DREAM

DREAM BIG
DON'T LET OTHER PEOPLE'S LIMITATIONS
BECOME YOUR REALITY

DREAM OFTEN
DON'T LET DISAPPOINTMENTS OF THE PAST
BECOME BLUEPRINTS OF THE HERE AND NOW

DREAM IN VIVID COLOR
DON'T LIMIT YOUR IMAGINATION
BY LIMITING YOUR THOUGHT PROCESS

DREAM LIKE A CHILD
EMBRACE THE FACT THAT DREAMS CAN BE
THE FORESIGHT INTO THE FUTURE
THROW CAUTION TO THE WIND
AND BELIEVE IN THE UNBELIEVABLE

DREAM
        JUST DREAM
                    DREAM OFTEN
                    DREAM IN VIVID COLOR
        DREAM LIKE A CHILD
    DREAM

DROWNIN'

I am going down
for the third time
I feel myself
slippin' away from
reality
from what I have come
to rely on
what I have come to
know
I don't want to be
saved
I don't want CPR
No mouth-to-mouth
I want to drown in
your love
be engulfed by your
embrace
smothered with your
kisses
as I go down for the
last time
I am NOT afraid
I know I will end up in
a better place
FOREVER
with you!

EMOTIONAL

I am an emotional fool
I feel everything so deeply; my whole being is moved
I am an emotional junkie
I feel to be alive, to remind myself that I am made up of more than just bones and blood
I am an emotional rollercoaster
Up, down, sideways, 180, 360, corkscrew of feelings spilling out in ways I least expect or in ways I can't control
When things come out of me in a way that can't be explained, not even to myself in a rational manner, I don't label, I learn to accept
Emotional doesn't equate crazy
Emotional is allowing you to be yourself by staying in the moment and not changing a thing
Those hiding behind their feelings have a difficult time understanding our plight
Our plight of not going insane but embracing the hard to grasp
I am part of a movement working towards being emotionally free
It takes dedication, long hours, and a heavy dose of honest reflection
The paycheck isn't big, but the rewards and benefits are endless
I am an emotional FOOL
And I wouldn't have it any other way
Working on myself is a daily process and I am the architect

FASHIONISTA

Those pants
Which match that blouse
Which perfectly falls in line with that new pair
of to-die-for shoes
makes you a fashionista

Knowing what to wear
to what party
and for what occasion
during any particular season
makes you a fashionista

By understanding your body type,
you know what looks good on you
By not condemning your body and
embracing your imperfections,
you are able to enhance your assets
Makes you a fashionista

Always wanting to look your best; not just
acceptable. Settling for nothing less than perfection
everyone who is anyone asking for your fashion
advice and you having your finger on the pulse of
the fashion scene, accommodates their every whim
without ever breaking a sweat because the one
who has great taste plus great style
is DEFINITELY
and will always be a
FASHIONISTA!

FEEL GOOD

YELL

    CURSE
Scream at the top of your lungs

Laugh

    Skip
Smile, showing all of your pearly whites

Speak directly to your inner child
by
using your inner voice
Reaffirming your greatest qualities over
and over again until you begin to believe them
yourself

Cry

Throw the ultimate tantrum

Let your feelings explode

Truly

    Feel

        GOOD!

FEMALE

Soft Skin
        Ruby Lips
                Mischievous Glance, Girlish Giggle
                        Flirtatious Walk, Come Hither Stance

Tall, Lanky, Lean Body
      Short, Petite, Small Frame
           Voluptuous Curves, Hourglass Figure

Willowy Blonde
        Brunette Bombshell
Fiery Redhead

Sweet Smell of Lingering Perfume
      High Heels Tapping on the Concrete
Slim-fitting Dresses Caressing Every Feminine Curve
      Pretty Faces Enhanced by Kisses from the Sun

Girl

        Woman

                Female

FRIENDSHIP

My friend, do anything for, die to the end, friend
Isn't it amazing how a simple "hi" could turn into a friendship for a lifetime?
The strongest shoulders I know to lean on when things get rough
The sweetest words to hear from someone who truly cares
Opinionated for my own good; to keep me out of trouble
Being silly to keep the laughs flowing and the tears to a minimum
My friend, tell anything to, go to the grave with, friend
There are people who come into your life for a reason and don't leave because
You need them
You are that person to me
My friend

FROM MY MOUTH TO YOUR EAR

From my mouth to your ear
Words that come alive when they are spoken
Words that have meaning when read aloud
Words that touch a place where nothing else
will fit

From my mouth to your ear
Whispered in a way that gives you a
comforting feeling
Words that surround you in a way that
make you feel safe
Make you feel you are protected, safe
from harm

Words which seem to form a song when
Linked to sentences that flourish when they
Reach the heart
Words that make you complete, make you
Whole
Words said to lift you up so floating is
Second nature

From my mouth to your ear
Spoken to you so you can hear!

HATE

Where does this feeling come from?

Is it learned?

Did we get it from our Daddy's, daddy's, daddy?

Did one wrong look from someone who's different from us, looks funny to us, give us the RIGHT to assume they will do some type of harm to us?

Does not knowing someone's origin make him or her a threat?

Does standing out in a crowd make that person a "marked man"?

Does a group matching that same person's color description make them inferior due to certain circumstances?

Does one generation's feelings against another generation justify their disgust for the other?

Does carrying on that deep disgust make it right just because your mother said so?

How can differences between races turn into something so ugly?

How can HATE rule the thoughts of so few while ruining the lives of so many?

HEART

When you have given of your heart over and over again,
Are you ever afraid it will never be returned whole?
When you have loved so much until it hurts, will you ever
Allow yourself to be put on the line again?

Have a heart, not a slab of stone

Open your arms wide enough so you won't close them out of
Vindictiveness
By accepting what you have pushed aside only allows positivity
To enter
By having a heart, you are able to see the heart in others
Goodness comes in many shapes and sizes and by opening
Yourself up to these possibilities only broadens your
Horizons of happiness
Both giving and receiving joy

HEAVY ON MY MIND

Life trying to handle you in any way possible
Delivering a crushing blow in the first round
Down, but definitely **NOT** out
A bruised ego is better than a **TKO**
Being taken out of the game means your opinions
Have no merit, nothing to stand on, no firm foundation
To build dreams on

Waking up in the middle of the night, in a cold sweat
Weighing heavy on my mind the fact that I am losing time by wasting energy
on things in which I have no control but thinking over time I will break the
mold, wear down that event which scares me, stare fear in the face

Good idea, by no means feasible!

Instead of taking on everything, pick and choose your battles
Life is short enough as it is, don't cut your time by making rash, quick
judgements

Weighing heavily on my mind what I want out of this life, at this time
Wanting what is best for myself and by doing better I am a better individual
The world is made up of many types of characters
Be the one who can win an Academy Award for best performance under
extreme circumstances

HOPEFUL

To Whom It May Concern:

We are writing to you, a concerned individual, for support and guidance. We are your down-trodden, the forgotten ones, the abandoned children, the beaten wives, the alcoholics, the drug addicts, the homeless, the mentally challenged, the pregnant teens, the juvenile delinquents, the misfits, the misunderstood, the less fortunate who have to rely and depend on a society that refuses to recognize us as whole beings; living amongst them in their community. We are raising our voices in a harmonious cry. Will you HELP us; can you be our VOICE, our LAST chance to be included, to be counted?

Signed,
Hopeless

Dear Hopeless,

Yes. I am a concerned individual, BUT I am not your Savior. You should rally together because you have rights as citizens and you need to be included amongst the masses. You are not to be walked on, spit on, ridiculed or discounted. When you begin to place yourself in higher esteem, others will begin to see you in the same light. By taking a stand on your own battles, others WILL know you mean business. By standing up and demanding that you be counted, to be recognized as part of society, no one can help but to notice you. Hopeless, I believe you are HOPEFUL!

Signed,
Someone Who Cares

HOW DOES IT FEEL

How does it feel to know that someone is always looking out for you?

How does it feel to have all of your fears under control?

How does it feel to be loved unconditionally, faults and all?

How does it feel to know joy beyond your wildest dreams?

How does it feel to be engulfed in comfort all the days of your life?

How does it feel to know that there is one person who will never let you down, no matter how low you feel you are?

How does it feel to know that whatever you need any time of day is just a prayer away?

I ask you again, how does it feel to be loved by an awesome Power? There are not enough words, not enough stars in the night, not enough grains of sand to describe how one person can touch so many at one time

All I can say is,"He is amazing!"

HYPOCRITE

Am I true to myself?
Do I say what I mean?
Mean what I do?
Do what I say?

Am I real to those around me?
Do I allow them to see the 'real' me?
Allow them to get close enough to view?
Do I even know who the 'real' me is?
If so, do I like what I see?

As I look in the mirror
I see a reflection
I see a figure, an image
As I look in the mirror
I think I catch glimpse of myself
Or is it the hypocrite in me
Seeing what I want to see
How I want to see it

I Love Me Some You

I just want to say to you, "I love me some you"
You are there in time of need, also when you need some time
You are heaven on earth, my guardian angel, someone that watches over me
You are very easy on my eyes and I am so thankful you are in my life
I knew you would be a great fit, the last piece to this puzzle called my life
I just want to say to you, "I love me some you", and I hope you feel the same

IF

If I asked you to be mine
to devote all your time and love to me, would you?
If I asked you to be faithful and put no female before me, could you?
Wanting you more than life itself
Wanting to love you more than wanting to take breath, is my current curse
Wanting you to make me yours, is a feat I am willing to endure
Waiting for you to commit to me is a sentence I am willing to live out
If I were the last woman on earth, would you not run straight into my arms,
declaring your undying love for me?
As I wait patiently, pretending you have seen the light, pretending you have
come to your senses, I wait alone
When I see you out and about, arm-in-arm with someone instead of me,
I close my eyes and envision the two of us, walking in a love-filled haze,
oblivious to the world around us
As my eyes open, I realize nothing had changed, same place, same position
as before – alone
If only…

INNOCENCE LOST

Innocence	Not making our own
Taken	Sick intentions
Without a	A reality
Second glance,	Why put those types
Without any	Of emotions on a
Type of conscience	Child
Ouch	Why take their small
That hurts	Power away from them
No one is	Why make them
Supposed to	Inferior for the rest of
Touch me	Their lives
There	
Especially	A place they ended up
With that	Because of the selfish
Don't do	Wanting of sick adults
That again!	Taking something precious
I'm gonna	Because an adult wouldn't
Tell	Give them any type of play
No sense of	Ouch
Decency	That hurts!
No sense of	Don't do that!
Obligation	I'm gonna tell!
Of protecting	What they REALLY
Our young	Want to say is
An oath taken by adults	DON'T take my

To look out for our children	Childhood away for your
Making sure	Sick pleasure
Their best interests	MASTURBATE!
Are taken into account	

INNUENDO

Remarks made to be mean
Degrading
Humiliating

How am I able to hold my head up high?
To walk the street with a confident attitude,
Without feelin' weighed down, without the watchful
Eye of doubt burning a hole in my back?

Make the innuendoes go away, STOP!
Take back whatever you said about me, whatever was insinuated
And return things back to normal
Or
At least back to what I know normal to be

The day I feel myself without second-guessing those around me
which includes you, is the day in which I regain a sense of control

If there is to be any criticism let it be correcting not damning

INSTIGATE

Why do I always start trouble?
Stir up something
Wreak havoc
Start shit
Why do I feel the need to be in the middle of mess?
The master of meddling
Saying things that I know will be the beginning of the end
Thinking that it's fun to witness others go at it
Instigating a fight
Starting nothing to see something jump off
Not realizing that by provoking trouble only
Ignites an instigation against me,
The originator of shit in the first place
Funny how events come full circle
Without any forewarning to the players of an imaginary game

LIFE CHANGE

Life long dream of
making it big in L.A.
Tinsel town
Land of broken dreams

Caught a Greyhound bus today Leaving behind
disappointments of the past, leaving behind my
old life for a new life of excitement, a life where
dreams can be played out in their entirety

Making new resolutions which can not only be
fulfilled, nor forgotten Finally reaching the
destination promised – a bus terminal to let out
the masses; persons wanting to cash in on their
dreams, not knowing what the future holds, but
knowing if they don't take a chance, the moment
will be lost forever

A country girl from Small-town, USA Eyes wide
open to the possibilities of fame Caught up in the
whirlwind of glamour of wanting to be a star,
wanting so badly to fit in, to be noticed
Many will come; many hearts will be broken, many
will lose faith quickly; even with the knowledge of
broken dreams and empty promises of fame, everyday
people step off the Greyhound bus thinking, hoping
they will beat the odds; thinking, hoping they will be
the next SUPERSTAR!

LITTLE POND

A fish who grew too big for the pond
In which you were supposed to be able
To spread out your fins

Wanting so desperately to find your
Way without selling your soul to the
Highest bidder or losing yourself in the
Shuffle, the madness

Wanting to fit in
Wanting to be independent
Wanting to do so simultaneously

Big fish, little pond
The world so vast
Until you have a chance to live in it
And are required to exist amongst
The land of the living

Thrown into the deep end and expected
To swim
Expected to survive in the environment
You were placed in to thrive

LIVIN' LARGE

Staking your claim
Markin' your territory
Knowin' whose block it is

Make sure you get your hustle on
By collecting all you are owed at once
One slip-up and you're out
Out of the game
No more duckets for you
No flexing your muscle
For all to see
Only shame and humiliation if you fail;
Fail to deliver the goods

These type of hard fastened commandments
May dictate fast life on the streets but they
Shouldn't be able to RULE you

Live large by getting an education
Live large by graduating Summa Cum Laude
Live large by working with honest people and earning legitimate money

Life is a gamble
With winners and losers
But before you end up behind the 8-ball too early in the game by becoming
bigheaded
Please stop and weigh all of your options, keeping in mind that just 'cause
something is pretty doesn't mean it can't turn ugly and
Just 'cause something is cool to the touch doesn't mean it can't get HOT
and burn

LOVE IS...

Love is freeing
Love is all seeing, all knowing
Love sees no color lines
Love sees no age differences
Love sees no gender

Love is feeling

Love can hurt
Love can also heal

Love is what you want it to be
because
LOVE is all encompassing

LOVE YA LIKE A PLAY COUSIN

Have you ever received an invitation late to a party
Or not at all then asked why you weren't there

Been told to your face the importance of embracing
Someone else's point of view

Been brushed aside by a friend then have that same
Friend ask you for a favor

Been the punch line of a joke which you didn't get but
Everyone around you was laughing

Gone out on a limb to find out you were the only one
On the branch

Being asked your opinion just to find out it really didn't
Matter to begin with

Thinking you look very sharp in a new outfit until someone
Points out your look is "SO YESTERDAY"

If any of these scenarios sound familiar or have happened
To you
Don't be alarmed
It just states what you already know, those who know you

Love ya like a play cousin!

LURE

Tiger's eye drawn to the flicker of the flame
A moth tries to fight the attraction but finds
Itself in the middle of the orange haze

A fly trapped in a spider's web; the sad thing
Being that the fly could be free but couldn't resist
The temptation of trying to outsmart the spider;
As the spider watched from a close distance the trap he had laid out,
he knew the fly's stupidity would out weigh his willingness to stay alive

Hypnotized by what we're attracted to; obsessed with things we have
no business having our eyes on; Convincing ourselves moment to
moment of how good it would make us feel to have what we desire,
what we want

LURE – to entice someone out in the 'wild' or the 'concrete jungle';
to seek out the weak ones and bring them back to us; to be savvy and
cunning without tipping your hand or showing you are bluffing by
hopefully not getting caught

LURE

    Gift

        Or

           Curse

MALE

Baby face, puppy dog eyes
Muscular build, sheepish grin
Lean body, GQ style

Blue collar, white collar, no collar, rough neck, scrub, pimp daddy, gigolo, family man, one-woman man

Bald-headed, crew cut, fade, Afro, cornrows, dreads, braids, twists

Loving, intense, misunderstood, hard-working, hustler, bread-winner, mamma's boy, faithful, gentle giant

Baggy pants
Three-piece suit
Kangol
Creased jeans
Chuck Taylors

Whatever your flavor, there's a male out there to fit the bill – just keep your eyes open to the possibilities!

ME

What is so special about me?
What is the big deal about little 'ol me,
everyday, nine-to-five, may blend into
any type of crowd me?
What makes me stand out more than anyone
else asking these very same questions?

I'll tell you why
I'll make a believer out of you to why I
am different from the rest

I am special because I was told I was
I am strong because I was taught to be
I stand out because I want to be seen
I do because I believe I can
I want because I believe I deserve
I work hard to be my personal best
I give of myself so others won't have to

Me
A simple word with such a huge burden to
carry if taken seriously

Me
carrying the load because I know what 'ME'
is capable of doing and becoming

MURPHY'S LAW

Why, when given the chance to step up to the plate – some people take the low road or no road at all?
Why, when given the chance to tell the truth – people decide to lie?
Why, when you find Mr. or Mrs. Right – one person does something to mess it ALL up?
Why, when you have done something wrong – you want the other person to apologize first?

With so many stipulations placed on how we should do things – is there any wonder why people have hidden agendas?
Hidden agendas about love
Hidden agendas about sex
Hidden agendas about one's self

Wanting and waiting
Differs from wanting and doing nothing
Wishing and hoping
Differs from not having any dreams at all

Live with the hand you were dealt with by LIVING

MY HERO

You can leap my heart in a single bound
Without making a sound
You can vaporize my ever-changing moods
Without breaking a sweat
You can use your ultra-violet rays to see right
through my schemes and lies
You can use your heat sensors to seek out my
True feelings with regards to you
With all the powers you possess and the extreme
Tactics you can use to figure out how people
Feel about you
I am here to let you know none of your powers
Are useful
You are my hero due to your heart
You are my hero due to your sweet nature
You are my hero due to your forgiving manner
You are my number one because of the fact
You love me and I am head-over-heels in love
with you
My Lois Lane to your Clark Kent
My vixen to your Superman
My hero, close enough to touch but dark enough
To be intriguing
By taking off both our masks we can explore
The beauty of a true relationship, faults and all

NAKED

Baring your soul
You, under the microscope
Every cell, super-exposed
While you have nothing to prove, you were
afraid that without saying a single word
one long, deep, hard look will unravel what you
tried so hard to keep hidden
revealing everything

What do you see in me?
How can I make you see what I have to offer?
What I am made of, what makes me whole
By baring parts of myself I don't even want
to admit exist
will prove to you how serious I am; serious about
my intentions; my intentions with regards to
you

As I stand naked before you, baring ALL
with no choice but to show my true self
I am stripped of everything, which could cloud
your judgement against me
I am transparent, see through, nowhere to hide
As I stand before you
I only have one question to ask –
Do you like what you see?

NOTHING ELSE SAID

Standing in the pouring rain
Waiting in the burning sun with no shade
Sleeping on your doorstep until you come home
Or
Until you invite me in

How many hints need to be hinted to?
How many chances given
How many times until the person gives in, gives into the demands of that
special someone

What will you do for the one you love?
Go to the ends of the earth without a map, without any directions readily
available
Enter a burning building, with no guarantee of making it out
The giving of your life to save theirs

What will you do for the one you LOVE?
Hopefully, everything you've done up until this point will have proven your
true devotion with no questions asked
No explanations needed

ON ANGELS' WINGS

Feelin' down and out
Feelin' like nothing is gonna change
I lift my eyes to the sky as my head hangs
down
On angels' wings
is where I place my prayers
to reach heaven and place at the feet of
The Father Almighty

Faith
Fluctuating in size from that of a mustard seed
to the size of a huge mountain which can stand
up to any type of weathering situation
Trust
is in abundance when things are goin' my way
but
becomes almost non-existent when my comfort
zone is tested
When life has to be lived, decisions made to the
best of my ability
Forgettin' who has always made a way for me
Attitude or not, no questions asked
On angels' wings
To guarantee the delivery of my prayers

On angels' wings
Having faith which is weightless but strong enough
To handle come what may

On angels' wings
A backbone, a springboard
to place my belief in Him

and make me to be the strong being
He created

God doesn't make mistakes
He makes miracles and I am
one of his original
masterpieces

POWER

Undisputed Greatness

Big Stick, low roar

Decisions made without haste

Made with precision

Always thinking of the common
Good

No ego boosting Firm without choking

Lenient without letting go

Mistakes made today
Become opportunities in the near
Future

Quiet
Undisputed Greatness
Is the
POWER
Of the here
And
Now!

RAY OF LIGHT

Sunshine peering through the blinds
A ray of hope
For those non-believers
That warmth can't burn through the darkness

Sunshine
Lighting up the noon sky
After a rain shower
Putting smiles on the faces of those who
Desperately seek happiness through outdoor
Exposure

You, a ray of light
My sunshine
Making me happier with each passing hour
Spreading more than what is expected
Giving of yourself
Completely to me
For my renewal, my awakening

REFLECTION

Seeing the opposite
Right is left, left is right
Seeing things one way, but is it the correct
way?

When we see ourselves in the glass as we pass,
Turning our head slightly to the side, is our image
Distorted or are we too rushed to see our true selves?

Pulling, tucking, pushing out, sucking in, making
shorter, standing taller
All done to give the impression of looking different,
Looking better

The illusion of how we want to be seen
As we quickly pass by the glass, turning our head
Slightly to the side, we see the reflection we want
Others to be envious of
The one which turns more than just heads

SACRIFICE

Sacrifice
A selfless act, done without malice
Without any expectations of being repaid
Doing something for the common good, to make
Someone feel his or her best
Doing something out of the ordinary which is
Unexpected but very much appreciated
Ultimate personal cost
Done without any thought, for loved ones
Considered an act of goodness when done for strangers
Considered a random act of kindness when done spontaneously
For someone who's totally unsuspecting but totally deserving
What would have the most impact?
What would make you sit up and take notice?
What would get the most attention, the most respect?
Something which is done for the good of the soul and the
Cleansing of the heart
Doing something that sets a positive example and if copied,
If continued, can change the world for the better

SAME LIKE ME

An unbreakable pair
Will do anything for each other
A love that is unconditional on both sides
Both, being mother and daughter

A role model
Someone not only to look up to but to truly
admire
A genuine beauty with brains to match
Someday I want to be just like her
Just like my mother

A younger version of myself
Fearless but also has an easiness about her
Wanting to still be nurtured but also knowing
She is a woman herself
Wanting approval, wanting to stand on her
own merits
My daughter, who is actually me I see

A tie that can't be broken
A bond that will not break
Mother and daughter
One the teacher, the other a willing student
absorbing all the knowledge which is laid out
in front of her by someone whom she trusts,
Someone who trusts her

Mother and daughter
Years may separate them but life experiences
Bring them closer than ever thought
Mother and daughter

The parent protecting her young by not
allowing her own ego to stifle her child's creativity
This act of pure love will not only carry her offspring
through the rough times but shine through the good
times as well

SAVE THE WORLD

Yes, I believe I can save the world
Save the world from everything that is going wrong
The backstabbing, jealousy, and envy of those
who have, still wanting more and will
Stop at nothing to get it
The ever growing divide between the have and
the have nots and the wedge which
Separates them for an eternity
Yes, I believe I can make a definite change due
to the mindset of those around me
Change comes about when something out of the
ordinary happens in the world of the
Mundane
Yes, I believe I can save the world by saving myself
Sometimes the simplest of plans proves to be the grandest of gestures

SHADES

Blacker the berry; sweeter the juice
Color of the ripest plum ready to be picked

High Priestess
Color of warm Caramel over cool ice cream

Cocoa Brown
Color of Dark Brown Sugar at the end of a strawberry for extra sweetness

Some call her Nubian Queen, Egyptian Princess, even Sapphire
Color of the brilliant blue stone with an attitude to match

Honey
Color of sunshine at dusk
Caribbean Goddess
Color of Espresso with cream

How you view or describe shades of women, from the blackest of the blacks
to the lightest of the browns, you encompass what it means to be a woman
of color
Not only proud of her heritage but prouder still that she is the spice of life
Spices that meet and compliment everyone's palate

SHE IS...

She is the reason why you wake up in the morning
The reason you have a skip in your step
She is the reason why you want the best and won't
settle for less because she brings the best out of
you
She is the reason why you take breath
because she has put life back into yours
She is the reason why you have a permanent
smile on your face, because hers is so contagious
She is the reason why you love life because she
loves you wholeheartedly without any hidden
agendas
She is the reason why you love yourself because
of the love poured out to you and you wanting to
share it
She is the all and all
She completes you and you her
Without one another, no half is whole
She is everything you had ever hoped she'd be
She is!

SHINE

A little elbow grease
A little effort to bring back the shine to your tarnished halo
Fallen from the pedestal where you were placed
Determined to get back into the good graces with those
You left behind
Without thinking, you went on a power trip, not taking
Any luggage on your adventure
Once there, you realized it's very lonely being where you
are
By doing some soul searching, personal inventory, individual
Housekeeping – inside and out
You are able to embrace what you were afraid of
GROWTH!

SING MY SOUL

Sing my soul a new song
Use my body by pulling on my heartstrings
Play my mind by laying out my life as if it were lyrics to the
hottest jam
Rhythms bouncing to the beat of my pounding heart
Sing my soul a new song
Wrap your arms around my waist like a baby would its blanket
Not only something to grab on to but something that won't
disappear if it is let go
Play my body like you would your favorite instrument knowin'
every finger strum, knowin' what comes next even before the note is played
Sing my soul a new song
One of hope and gladness; not one of glum and sadness
Make me blush like a young girl in love,
Reminiscing about her first REAL kiss
Make me blush like I am in love; in love with you
My soul is singin' a new song
A day is dawnin' a new morn
All for the sake of love
All for the fact you took the time to take someone out of tune and
placed them in the RIGHT key

Sistah Girl, Sistah Friend

Strong, beautiful, confident
Quick-witted, brutally honest
Tough exterior, heart of gold
Level-headed, sweetly affectionate
Focused yet abstract enough to be centered
Sharp tongue, great insight
Related not by blood but by race, which is one in the same

Sistah girl, sistah friend

Behind you unconditionally
Will drop you like a bad habit if you are purposefully deceitful
Always there in need, sight or sight unseen
Ready to throw down, but always elegant
Considers truth and commitment an oath

Sistah girl, sistah friend

God put you here for me and there aren't enough
thank you's for you as my gift

SKIN DEEP

The perfect pout
Lashes passing the point of
being legal, looking more like black
wings than something created with
a wand
Eyebrows arched with precision making
you look like the diva you really
are
Colors picked to showcase your beauty
Eyes made up in dramatic fashion
not to offset but to mesmerize everyone
around you
like they need any convincing
Foundation blended to hide any flaws, which
on you are a minimum
A healthy glow, which can't be captured in a
bottle
Only by living
Let those around you enhance your looks
Let good friends enhance your good complexion
because
Love brings out the best in all of us
With or without
Our protective armor

SMILE

Every thought I have of you makes me smile
When I hear your name, a smile is immediately
placed on my face
The way you make difficult things seem so easy
to do astonishes me
Even your corny jokes that you swear are hilarious,
tickle me in the sweetest way
The way you can fall asleep with the television on,
makes me laugh
The way you caress my face with your fingertips
not only excites me, it shows me that I am loved
I pray I never have to be without your warm touch,
your kind words or your love for me
By smiling, I know you are never far from me
You are the reason I believe in love, and I never
want that feeling to go away!
That's why I SMILE!

SOLITUDE

To be at peace with one's self
To be in a place where you feel comfortable; a
place you can retreat and feel safe
to be able to be alone without feeling lonely

How does one begin to gain peace within themselves?

How does one begin to become comfortable in their
own skin; begin to recognize they can retreat inward
to find what they are in search of?

To think of space, one may think of a place where
it is peaceful and serene Solitude can come from
a place of self discovery, self exploration – beginning
to familiarize one's self with how one feels or responds
to whatever is given to them in the way of living each
day

Self discovery, self-exploration is a great gift and
most of us are not aware of its awesome power until
we begin to embrace the fact that we are still in the
learning process until the day we no longer have
breath

To be at peace with one's self is to have a sense of solitude

SORRY FOR WHAT

Sittin' here thinkin'
Thinkin' of my Black Brothas, past and present
Thinkin' of my race, rich with wisdom and culture
Thinkin' about comments made about our race, things
I have heard about 'us' and the things we don't do

Obviously, the words I heard weren't uplifting nor
worth repeating

The day I realized the negativity was being directed at
My Black men, I stood up and took notice, a closer look
at the situation going on, were the comments TRUE to
some point?
Were there other solutions tried before doing what was
typically expected – doing the wrong thing
Come on, my Black Brothas, where are you?
You all can't be on the street corners slangin'; locked
Behind bars, filling the jails that are being built for you –
Near and far; cryin' 'cause ALL the good jobs are taken;
Still living in your mama's house past the age of 40; you
ALL can't be in these predicaments!
What happened to my strong Black Brotha – Head held
high, pride of the neighborhood, making a good and honest
living
Where did my Black Brotha go – No shrinking violet, a
Silhouette of a god
What happened to my silent partner – Never forgetting
Who you belong to or who loves you
What happened to my Black Brotha – where are you?
Where did you disappear to?

I didn't place the handcuffs on you, I didn't promise you
A pipe dream of easy money and no work, I didn't promise
To be with you so I could laugh at you and then leave
If you know I am NOT the ONE who placed you where
You are, what should I be sorry for? What do you think
I owe you?
ME, SORRY FOR WHAT?
Be the person I know and expect you to be by living up to
your potential
Make our race proud
Make yourself PROUD

SOUL FOOD

Letting sit, stew
Soaking up all the flavors
of your soul
Marinating, allowing your feelings
To permeate the air
Allowing your body to be infused by the
Sights and smells of everything which surrounds
you
Your scent, flowing through the air ever so gently
For all to experience
Marinate your being so you can explode with
Flavor
Engulfed with what life has to offer
Enjoying every delectable bite
Letting sit, stew
Soaking up all the flavors of your soul
Food for you to feed on so you can live off
Eternal bliss
Allowing love to be the source where good
Things are fueled
Food for the soul which can nourish us all
So we no longer hunger
Substance so we can grow
Grow from what we were taught to what we
know

SPEAK!

The stopwatch starts after uttering the word "HELLO"
We're encouraged to talk but are warned to limit ourselves to the Reader's Digest version – being as condensed as humanly possible; only hitting the highlighted points

With so much to say, we cram what we can into the time allotted, not caring much about the sense being made or the tone in which it is delivered

Is it any wonder why we question if we're being listened to? If people are really paying attention to the words we say or are they just waiting patiently until we shut up so they can have their turn to start their rambling?

The time clock of life is ticking, so watch your words carefully!

STILL

The still of my heart
Not beating so it won't wake my mind
My mind which tends to wander to negative events
The calm before the storm
Turbulence that happens when silence is broken
And is not returned to the state in which it was found
The still of my thoughts
So loud I would close my eyes to deaden the sound
Usually my mind races when it is faced with challenges
Beyond what I feel I am capable of accomplishing
Or
Am I at an advantage if I look at the situation differently?
The still of my actions
No motion, uttering no movement
I feel I am living in a dream, a dream with no real players
Only going through the motions of life
Only living when nothing is happening
The still of my being
Listening intently so I can connect with my whole
Existence

SUDDENLY

Why did you leave me so soon?
I was depending on you, you to make my life complete
Everything I needed you gave me
Moral support is what you were best at
Not letting me fall when I felt I was about to lose it
Didn't you know I needed you in ways you could hardly understand?
You believed in me and it seemed you could read my mind by doing things
correctly before I did them

Why did you leave me without any type of notice?
Didn't I deserve that much?
I bet that was the last thing on your mind, trying to let me down easily
I guess when I sit down and think about it; it was for the best
Leaving suddenly hurts less than dragging it out for a very long time
I was selfish because I wanted you around for what seemed to be forever
because I needed you in my life
I cried, bitched, and moaned to try and get you back, but I failed

The one thing I learned which you taught me that will stay with me for the
rest of my life is I can depend on myself in times of doubt
That I have a strong head on my shoulders and if I just use it, I not only can
surprise myself but those around me as well

SUNSHINE

What an eye opener
What a way to show your feelings, a true sentiment
A gesture, a kind word, a random act of kindness
A warm smile, inviting and sincere attached with your best interest in mind
Kind-hearted, not phony
Wanting what is good all around without thinking of any consequences, good or bad
Not being indifferent, but being real, being true
Taking a stand doesn't mean being confrontational
Investing in you doesn't mean being selfish
Wanting what is best doesn't have to be a negative
Surrounding yourself with better isn't being snobbish
Researching doesn't mean doubting
What a breath of fresh air!
What a way to express your feelings!
A sigh of relief, a feeling which is surrounded by that of comfort in an otherwise unsettling predicament

A ray of sunshine, a glimpse of light, that of hope which is sure to awaken our senses
Brightening up the state of affairs taking hold of our very existence

SHINE ON!

TEACH

Teach one to be independent
Teach one to be supportive
Teach one to experiment
Teach one to be more expressive
Teach one to achieve
Teach one to love
Teach one to respect others
Teach one to respect their self
Teach one to relax
Teach one to appreciate creativity
Teach one to take chances
Teach one to forgive
Teach one to be carefree
Teach one to stand up to adversity
Teach one to laugh
Teach one to embrace their beauty
Teach one to accept their faults
Teach one to accessorize
Teach one to flaunt their positives
Teach one to embrace life
Teach one by example

TEARS

As I wipe a tear from one of my cheeks, before it drops from my chin, I am
Reminded of happiness

My childhood
My first love
Then my mind wanders to sadness
My first failure
True heartache

By releasing my tears, I am shedding my old existence for a new one
A new life filled with adventure and excitement, not only for what has
happened
But thinking back to a more content time, a more solemn time
A bit scared about what lies ahead but growing more anxious with each passing
Moment

As I wipe a tear from one of my bottom lashes, I am reminded of life

THE "DO"

LONG, SHORT, WAVY, CURLY

SILKY, STRAIGHT, NAPPY, TANGLY

HIGH MAINTENANCE, LOW MAINTENANCE,
NO MAINTENANCE

FRIED, DYED, LAID TO THE SIDE

UP-DOS, BRAIDS, DREADS, AFROS, BOBS, TWISTS,
CURLS, SHAGS, CROPPED OR FEATHERED

HIGHLIGHTS, EXTENSIONS, WEAVES, WIGS

BLACK, BROWN, BURGUNDY, MAUVE, BLONDE

WHATEVER THE REASON, SEASON, DAY OR MOOD –
YOU CAN BEST BELIEVE THE "DO" WILL RISE TO
THE OCCASION AND BEAT THE EXPECTATION
OF THE WEARER

THE VERDICT

The perfect crime
or
so it seems
Flawless in its execution
Meticulous in its detailing
Justification
On the righting
of a wrong
The painful realization
of being betrayed
then lied to
brings about a tearful
confession followed up
by the ever convincing
plea for forgiveness
Condemning the actions
of the guilty party
by
giving yourself a
pardon to rid the
earth of wrong doers
comes with a price
Freedom
For a clear conscience
or
the perception of one

THE VOW OF MARRIAGE

The moment the "I do's" are said and the ceremony
over, the life of together begins
The "I's" become "we" and there is no more "me", yes
you are still an individual but your thoughts include
another person and their feelings as well
Love is what brought you two together and
commitment is what will keep you forever
As the years pass, hair will turn gray, wrinkles will set in, features will
change but in each other's eyes there is no one in the world who will
do but the one you're with and nothing will change that feeling
You know their every look, smile, sigh, or frown and
how to handle each one when they arise, like you know
your own moods and how to calm yourself down
No one said this journey would be easy but knowing the person beside
you loves you unconditionally puts you at ease like nothing else can
This person next to you has chosen to spend the rest of their life
in your arms, in your care, in your love until parted by death
No one can come between two so committed to each other, to
the vows made before God, the vows made to one another
What a beautiful thing to witness when the real thing
happens to those who take the process seriously, who
have found that one-in-a-million someone
The vow of marriage is not only putting up with the
bad, but rejoicing in the good, the fact that you will be
happy with this person for the rest of your days
By putting in the effort, the rewards are great
By staying in for the long haul, shows those just beginning
that the fairytale is real and does comes true
The vow of marriage is alive and well just by looking at the two of you

THEY TURN INTO ANGELS

The big question, the unsolved mystery is –
Where do our loved ones go when they die?
My belief, which is solely based on faith, is that the people we loved, who shared our lives for either a brief or extended amount of time, ascend into heaven and become our eyes and ears to the world

They protect us from ourselves
They become our unsung heroes, memories we bring to life so they are not forgotten
Flowers placed at the gravesites to bring their spirit back to life
Placing their urn atop of the fireplace to warm their soul

When our loved ones die, we don't quite understand but there is a divine plan in action
Our loved ones become angels
Guardian angels who serve God and protect our well being
Faith and hope in a promise made on a cross keeps our hearts strong
It doesn't ease the pain of loss, but we can rest assured that one day we too can join the chorus of those before us, singin' the praises of Our Lord
A choir of angels who had looked after us before we had our chance to ascend to our rightful place – side by side with them in full harmony

THOSE WHO...

Who benefits from LIES?
Those who tell them or
those who foolishly want to believe the
half-baked truths?

Does deceiving those
around you make you
feel big, larger than life,
important?

Spinning a web of deceit
can backfire
those who mislead can just
as easily be the misled

Don't think for a moment that the
LIES won't catch up with you

Remember,
what goes around will
DEFINITELY
come around

It is called "KARMA" and it will
ALWAYS bite you when you least expect it
At a time which is the most damning

THUMBS UP!

Do you want me to be happy for you?
Jump up and down?
Do a congratulatory dance?
Give you your props?

What do you want from me?
Do you want me to put my best face forward?
Put in a good word for you?
Say you were nothing but kind to me?
Wishing nothing but the best for you from here on out?
Hoping your future is bright and your next love brighter?

I guess it would be petty of me to be a woman scorned, but I am
It is unfortunate that things didn't work out for us
But for me to do an about face and hope you find the love of your life in this new person is out right ridiculous
What am I entitled to, what feelings do I have a right to express in this failed relationship?
I believe being angry, mad, or upset are the ones I can choose from, but giving you a "Thumbs Up!" isn't!

TOUCH

What I want from you most
What I can't seem to live without is that thing you do
Without any type of fore thought
Whether it be light, with pressure or totally on a whim
It makes me feel connected to you

That I am yours, someone you find difficult to move away from
Touch me, never let me go
Make me feel I am IT, the only one that matters, the only one you
want to see and the only one who sees you

Touch me ever so gently; make me quiver anticipating your next
move
Your move towards me
Touch me with your eyes
Because anything more at this time might be too much to handle

TRIUMPH

Those who know DO
Those who don't WON'T
Those who can't QUIT

Be one who will
Be one who can
Be the one who knows
better
Because you will DO
better

Anything else is
UNACCEPTABLE!

TRUST.... YOURSELF

Who knows you?
Who knows you better than
You know yourself
No one

Yes, people claim to have
Your best interests
At heart
Claim to know what is good
For you
But, when it comes right down to it
Other people may love you
But you know you!

Who do you put your trust in?
The love of your life, your family, your friends
Besides placing your trust in the Almighty
Who always has your heart on redial
Trust yourself, trust your judgement, and trust your instincts
God gave you a brain –
SO USE IT!

ULTIMATE

The way you kiss me
The touch of your warm breath against my neck
Makes me quiver with excitement
The anticipation of what will follow:

>   Your hands on my thighs
>   My breasts on your back
>   Your mouth on my stomach
>   My lips on your chest

Toes and legs wrapped around each other like snakes wrapped around
Tree branches melting into the background until they become one
One body moving in unison, the feeling of ecstasy as both mechanisms
Climax together
Feeling the pulse of the other person, waiting for the silence to sweep over
You both but too excited over the joy of being satisfied
Satisfied by the one you love
The one you have given yourself to
Completely!

UNBELIEVABLE

Your smile
The way your mouth curls when you laugh
The way your eyes sparkle looking into mine
Unbelievable

Your touch
The way you kiss me passionately
The way you make me feel when I am with you
Unbelievable

Your arms
The way you hold me tightly, not wanting to let go
The way I feel your love through your fingertips
Unbelievable

Your demeanor
The way you express your emotions
The way your feelings translate into words
Unbelievable

Your love
The way you give it unconditionally
The way everyone reacts to your generosity
Unbelievable

I am better for knowing you
I am a better individual with you in my life
Together we are unmistakably
Unbelievable

WHY ME?

I asked myself one day – why me?
Why am I always the one left out?
Why am I always feeling down?
Why am I not rich?
Why do I struggle from day to day?
Why am I not famous?

After a long deliberation – I asked myself a different question –
Why not me?
Why not me to make sure I feel included instead of excluded
Why not me to share my feelings instead of bottling them inside
I may not be rich with possessions, but I am very wealthy in self worth
Why not me to put in a hard day's work

Many dream of becoming famous or having their fifteen minutes of fame –
but why not me to be satisfied with the person I have become and be secure
in the fact that by staying true to what I believe in and the morals I have
makes me very famous indeed

YOU GRANDMOTHER

You
>   With a permanent smile on your face

You
>   Strong, confident and never yielding

You
>   Generous and ever so loving

You
>   The giver of life – four generations strong

You
>   In line with other determined Black women who made a difference

You
>   The Silent Cheerleader

You
>   The Backbone of the family

You
>   A friend to many because everyone wants to be close to you in some way,
>   Shape or form

You
>   Who was ALWAYS stylish and ever SO VAIN

You
>   Who wanted to stay young forever

You
>   Who sacrificed so much for the ones you loved and continued to do so
>   For their well being

You
>   With love overflowing and still more to spare

You
>   Who could bring strangers together and make them feel like family

You
>   One of the most beautiful women of the world

Many will be sad on this day with just cause, we lost someone very dear to our Hearts and to our soul

But you would say to ALL of us –
Stand straight, head held high, walk tall
This is my HOMECOMING and a day of CELEBRATION
Each ray of sunshine
Each sparkling twinkle in the night's sky is me looking down on ALL OF YOU –
SMILING!

YOU

As I lift my eyes
towards God
your blessings rain
down on me like manna
from heaven
As I fold my hands to pray
You answer my cry ten times
over
I never seem to be without
when You are in my midst
I never seem to be alone
when I am in your presence
I am your child because
You claimed me
I bow down to You because
You are King
I am made in your image because
You created me
I am because You are

ABOUT THE AUTHOR

Mrs. Fleming-Bendo has been writing poetry and short stories for a number of years. After participating in "open mic" events and other venues, there seemed to be a small group forming and individuals inquiring on how they could receive some of Mrs. Fleming-Bendo's work. The feedback to her poetry was it stood out from anything they had heard up to this date and wanted to hear more, preferably in written form. That's where the idea of creating a book of poetry came into play.

Michelle has a Bachelor's Degree in Psychology and a Master's Degree in Rehabilitation Counseling, emphasis in Drugs and Alcohol. She had been working in this particular field for about nine years before deciding to follow her passion of writing. To be able to put her words on to paper and for others to appreciate what she is doing by wanting to read more is a dream come true! Finally, all this hard work paid off, a book to call her own.

www.ingramcontent.com/pod-product-compliance
Lightning Source LLC
Chambersburg PA
CBHW020919140626
46545CB00015B/888